CW00868681

Understanding Knowledge Management

in a week

JOHN MACDONALD

Hodder & Stoughton

A MEMBER OF THE HODDER HEADLINE GROUP

Acknowledgements

The author and publisher would like to thank the following for their assis-
tance in the preparation of this book and permission to quote from their work:
David J. Hutchinson, Bower & Company, recruitment specialists in knowledge
management (0171 929 5040)
Nigel Osborn, Managing Director of TFPL Ltd., international KM consultants
(0171 251 5522)
Robin Walker, Managing Director of The Performance Improvement Group,
management consultants (01386 40703)
Chris Davies, BT's Knowledge management team (0171 778 5300)

Oxford University Press for the figures on pages 20 and 21 taken from
*The Knowledge Creating Company: How Japanese Companies Create the Dynamics of
Innovation* by Ikujiro Nonaka and Hirotaka Takenchi.
Copyright © 1995 by Oxford University Press, Inc.

Orders: please contact Bookpoint Ltd, 39 Milton Park, Abingdon, Oxon OX14
4TD. Telephone: (44) 01235 400414, Fax: (44) 01235 400454. Lines are open from
9.00 - 6.00, Monday to Saturday, with a 24 hour message answering service.
Email address: orders@bookpoint.co.uk

British Library Cataloguing in Publication Data
A catalogue record for this title is available from The British Library

ISBN 0 340 757868

First published 1999
Impression number   10 9 8 7 6 5 4 3 2 1
Year   2005 2004 2003 2002 2001 2000 1999

Copyright © 1999 John Macdonald

Typeset by Multiplex Techniques Ltd, St Mary Cray, Kent.
Printed in Great Britain for Hodder & Stoughton Educational, a division of
Hodder Headline Plc, 338 Euston Road, London NW1 3BH by Cox & Wyman
Ltd, Reading, Berkshire.

in *the Institute of Management*

The Institute of Management (IM) is the leading organisation for professional management. Its purpose is to promote the art and science of management in every sector and at every level, through research, education, training and development, and representation of members' views on management issues.

This series is commissioned by IM Enterprises Limited, a subsidiary of the Institute of Management, providing commercial services.

Management House,
Cottingham Road,
Corby,
Northants NN17 1TT
Tel: 01536 204222;
Fax: 01536 201651
Website: http://www.inst-mgt.org.uk

Registered in England no 3834492
Registered office: 2 Savoy Court, Strand,
London WC2R 0EZ

━━━ C O N T E N T S ━━━

Knowledge management is emerging as a key management tool for the new century. To achieve a sustained competitive advantage management need to understand, implement and support a new competence throughout the organisation: the ability to manage knowledge effectively.

Knowledge management is the process of making creative, effective and efficient use of all the knowledge and information available to an organisation for the benefit of its customers and thus the company. Knowledge is therefore an intellectual asset which in the new global economy will become more important than the traditional capital assets.

This is not a new concept as this book will demonstrate but the recent advance of communication technologies provides an easier opportunity to acquire, codify and distribute knowledge more effectively. To provide the leverage to turn this knowledge to competitive advantage organisations need to create a cultural environment in which information and knowledge is shared, managed and used.

The aim of the book is to provide a step-by-step guide to the understanding of knowledge and its effective use. The week ahead comprises:

Sunday	Understanding the principles
Monday	Developing a learning culture
Tuesday	Setting the direction
Wednesday	Defining how to go about it
Thursday	Using technology
Friday	Adapting and using knowledge
Saturday	What it means to the individual

The power of knowledge

Knowledge has always been seen as power. It can be used for the good of many or the wealth of the few. So knowledge has always been sought, and if not found it is invented, or the existing knowledge is altered and then called faith. Throughout history the proprietors of knowledge and the protectors of faith have fought to control and ration the dispersal of knowledge. Business has tended to exhibit the same attitudes to knowledge. With modern technology, such control has become increasingly difficult and, indeed, counterproductive in business.

Since the middle of the last century, scientific and technical advances have enhanced the ability of diverse civilisations and cultures to communicate and expand shared knowledge. The converging development of railways, steamships, automobiles and airplanes has provided global mobility. Large numbers of people now regularly move outside their familiar environments. This exposure to different value systems and social behaviour is altering the perceptions of customers, employees and all involved in business around the world. Now new telecommunications and information technology is accelerating the process of change. At the same time it has also helped to create the global market and provide new opportunities to exploit the power of knowledge for a sustained competitive advantage.

Businessmen and financiers have long embraced advances in communications capabilities to capture and distribute information to their competitive advantage. The semaphore was used to bring early information of the defeat of Napoleon at Waterloo to make a killing on the London financial market. Samuel Morse sent the first telegraph message in 1844 which quickly replaced the semaphore and, as a result, Associated Press was founded in New York, soon followed by the formation of the Western Union Telegraph Company. Baron de Reuter used the telegraph and pigeons to link telegraph stations at national boundaries, thus creating the first information network. He founded Reuter's news service to sell financial, political and general information to European newspapers in 1849.

So by the middle of the last century entrepreneurs had recognised that the acquisition and speedy distribution of information, allied to the knowledge of how to do it, represented a new capital asset with which to build great businesses. By 1875 Alexander Graham Bell had developed the telephone and by the turn of the century Guglielmo Marconi had demonstrated wireless telegraphy and the radio, though we had to wait until 1925 before

John Logie Baird unveiled television. Finally, following the Second World War, the computer became a practical commercial asset.

The next fifty years saw the development and convergence of these technologies to provide the opportunities for what is now called the 'Information age'. New entrepreneurs have recognised the power of this knowledge to build new empires which rival the great giants of the nineteenth Century. Bill Gates, Rupert Murdoch and Ted Turner are this era's equivalent of Rockerfeller, Carnegie and Hearst.

Business has not been isolated from this whole movement. They have sought information to use it as knowledge to enhance their performance. Competitive intelligence, industrial espionage and benchmarking are aspects of this striving for knowledge. But this is an emphasis on gaining or acquiring *external* knowledge. There is now a growing awareness of the vast array of knowledge that exists within the organisation. This knowledge is derived from many sources and much of it is latent and unexploited. Slowly, business is beginning to realise that this knowledge represents intellectual capital which if it can be released and used is the most important asset available to a company in creating and retaining a competitive edge. The intellectual or intangible asset of knowledge is now a capital asset which is becoming more important than the traditional assets of facilities, equipment and products.

This awareness of the importance of internal knowledge has coincided with, or been sparked by, the growth and widespread availability of affordable information technology. This now provides the capability to collect, codify, analyse, combine, store, develop and disseminate knowledge throughout the organisation. The information age can be succeeded by the knowledge age.

Knowledge management

The awareness of the value of intellectual capital has begun to concentrate management minds on the ways to release this powerful potential. Peter Drucker, a famed management guru, was the first to draw attention to this area more than twenty-five years ago, since when a host of other management thinkers and pioneering companies have taken the lead in developing thought and practice in this element of business. At the same time, Western leaders began to recognise that as with quality management the Japanese had 'been there first'. Now these experiences are being combined to provide a collective theoretical and practical base to assist all those organisations who have the will to change and adapt.

A combination of management awareness, attitudes and practices, systems, tools and techniques designed to release the power of knowledge have emerged from the initial phases. This combination is called **Knowledge management.**

The aim of this book is to help develop a clear understanding of this combination so that many organisations can adapt, rather than adopt, the techniques described to their own unique situation. As with all previous management theories there is abundant evidence that some organisations have taken the 'quick fix' route. To be successful in the long term organisations should see knowledge management as a business evolution rather than an information technology revolution.

What is knowledge?

If we are intent on managing knowledge we need to be clear about what we mean by the word *knowledge*. Theory and experience have demonstrated that, from a management perspective, there are clear distinctions between two types of knowledge. Common practice now refers to them as *explicit* and *tacit* knowledge. They can be described as follows:

- Explicit knowledge is precisely and clearly expressed, with nothing left to implication. Generally in the business situation it is fully stated and openly expressed without reservation.
- Tacit knowledge is understood but not clearly expressed. It is often personal knowledge embedded in individual experience and involves intangible factors, such as personal belief, perspective and values.

We need to develop the characteristics of these sectors of knowledge to understand how they can be managed.

Explicit knowledge
Companies hold substantial documented knowledge in patents, technical specifications and procedures. Additionally, information is routinely collected, stored and distributed as management information. Financial, marketing, production, and service information is usually codified and is ready for different distribution channels.

This information makes up the majority of explicit knowledge.

All of this information has value in its own right and in most organisations could be used more effectively. There is also a need to seek even more explicit knowledge in the daily conduct of business. There is a readily available source of this knowledge in all communication with customers, suppliers, distributors, competitors, the community and government agencies.

Tacit knowledge
The most valuable asset of every organisation is the hidden or tacit knowledge buried in the memories of employees and other *people* in regular contact with the organisation. This experience includes learning from doing as well as study, observation and informal information or even gossip.

By definition this is more difficult to both recognise and collect let alone codify, store and distribute. Yet this is the key component of knowledge management. Releasing the true potential of this asset on a continuous basis involves far more than the capability of information technology.

The management of knowledge

The management challenge is to capture and combine both these elements of knowledge to spark innovation so as to create *new knowledge*, i.e. a new asset that can be employed to improve or to produce new products and services that will achieve a sustained competitive advantage. We will return to the creation of knowledge later today.

Managing this transformation *will* involve investing in the latest information technology (IT) and will require the supporting competence of IT skills throughout the organisation. But to rely on sophisticated technology alone to release the potential of knowledge in the company is to court disaster. Management must recognise that the main priority is to develop an operating culture that is conducive to participatory communication.

On Monday we will focus on how to develop a learning culture which is directed at this aspect of knowledge creation. Later in the week we will return to the theme of a working environment that encourages innovation and supports the trust that is needed to ensure the natural sharing of personal knowledge. Knowledge management in the corporation is akin to the performance of a great orchestra. Every member of the orchestra has a tacit knowledge of how to use their instrument (or element of technology) to produce a great individual sound. The conductor (chief knowledge officer – CKO) combines this tacit knowledge with a specific knowledge of the score to produce a harmonious combination that is greater than the sum of the individual sounds.

A word of warning
Some companies, in their eagerness to stay ahead, are falling victim to the IT trap. Listening to the siren voices of IT consultants, they are investing heavily in networking systems (intranet) and data warehousing without paying sufficient attention to the cultural aspects of human behaviour.
To quote the comedian, it's 'déjà vu all over again'!

Management's obsession with the quick fix, driven by short term financial considerations, has resulted in the relative failure of many previous initiatives such as total quality management, process re-engineering and employee empowerment. As before, successful knowledge management will require:

- comprehension before commitment
- recognition and ownership of need
- time for thought and planning rather than instant action
- adaptation rather than adoption of new concepts
- constancy of purpose.

This book is designed to support these requirements.

Why go to all this trouble?

Management are increasingly aware of the potential advantages of harnessing the skills and knowledge of their employees. Many factors have contributed to this growing awareness. They include the advent of the global economy and increased competition, the growing intellectual content of products and services and the organisation's dependence on knowledge workers and the ready availability of relatively inexpensive information technology.

Knowledge management is seen as a way of achieving competitive advantage through:

- *Better product performance* – knowledge of what has happened instigates product and service improvements
- *Faster reaction to changing markets* – greater knowledge of the changing perceptions of customers and interdepartmental collaboration through communication will bring new responses and products to the market in greatly reduced timescales

- *Substantial reduction in wasted effort and resources* – open and shared communication by empowered employees will eliminate the problems and roadblocks that hamper smooth production and delivery
- *Innovative breakthroughs* – the continuous combination of explicit and tacit knowledge will create a spiral of knowledge that will result in totally new answers to market needs and organisational performance
- *Dedicated workforce* – enhancing employees' sense of worth and involvement will bring a new era of employee/employer relationships.

Intellectual capital

We have already noted the growing importance of intellectual capital. Shareholders have long recognised this fact, even if only intuitively. For company management this is bringing a new perspective to the management of people. In retrospect we can see that *total quality management* was the catalyst that started this new approach.

A company's stock market capitalisation, the price of its shares or the price paid when it is taken over or sold as a going concern, is often more than the declared tangible asset value, as seen in the annual report and accounts. The difference, the intangible asset value or intellectual value, is fundamentally a valuation of a company's competence to continue to succeed at its business – the value of goodwill, its market brand and its knowledge base.

This intellectual capital represents a growing proportion of market value. For many hi-tech or high brand value companies this represents over 90% of their market value, and in a few cases over 100% – famously, the tangible assets of Microsoft, for example, are a very small proportion of its market value.

The management of intangible assets has received relatively little attention in the business world but as the value of knowledge becomes more widely accepted the definition and measurement of intellectual capital is gaining focus. The accounting profession has taken a very cautious approach to working intangibles into company accounts but is considering new standards.

What can't be measured, can't be managed, so knowledge management is now playing a major part in developing this new financial discipline. A recent book *Intellectual Capital – Navigating the New Business Landscape* by Roos, Roos, Dragonetti and Edvinsson develops this whole area with new insights into measuring intellectual capital.

But perhaps more significant for the future of business is that the focus on the value of knowledge is bringing a new focus on the value of people. For years executives have parroted the phrase 'our people are our greatest asset' while giving very little practical evidence that they really meant it. The measurement of intellectual capital will mean that in future management really will see people as their greatest asset.

HE MADE US
2 BILLION LAST
WEEK

Organisational knowledge creation

A number of leaders in management thinking, starting with Peter Drucker more than 20 years ago, have contributed to the current development of knowledge management. But with the publication of their book *The Knowledge Creating Company* in 1995, two Japanese professors Ikujiro Nonaka and his colleague Hirotaka Takeuchi proclaimed a theoretical base for organisational management of knowledge.

The book seeks to demonstrate how Japanese companies create the dynamics of innovation and provides a critical comparison between the attitudes of western and Japanese management to knowledge. According to Nonaka, western management sees the organisation as a machine for information processing while Japanese management concentrates on the creation of knowledge rather than knowledge itself. The authors focus on knowledge as a competitive resource and represent this business strategy as:

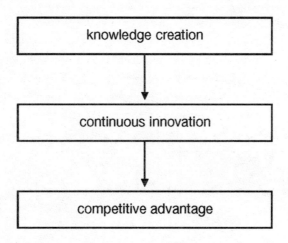

The criticism of western management has some validity but the examples in the book do not fully support their thesis. But the real value of the book is its powerful intellectual model for the dynamic interplay between explicit and tacit knowledge to create knowledge. It describes four modes of knowledge conversion as illustrated in the figure below:

Tacit knowledge *to* Explicit knowledge

Tacit knowledge	**Socialisation**	**Externalisation**
from		
Explicit knowledge	**Internalisation**	**Combination**

Four modes of knowledge conversion

- *Socialisation* – sharing information with others. This means more than just talking, and involves sharing internal knowledge and insights in a structured manner. Related to how the apprentice learns from the master craftsman.
- *Internalisation* – learning by doing and creating tacit knowledge from specific knowledge.
- *Externalisation* – the ability to look outside and envisage something better and different; the basis for innovation.
- *Combination* – this mode is a process of systemising concepts into a knowledge system. This conversion involves combining different bodies of explicit knowledge.

The spiral of knowledge

The four modes of knowledge provide a model to help understanding and to assist with the implementation of a knowledge management initiative. But the modes remain static statements unless we can *manage* an interaction between the discreet modes.

We noted that socialisation aims at the sharing of tacit knowledge. But until it can be converted into specific knowledge it cannot be codified, distributed throughout the organisation and then leveraged to create new knowledge. Moreover, a series of discreet pieces of tacit or explicit knowledge, even when combined, does not extend the organisation's value base. Organisational knowledge creation demands a continuous and dynamic interaction between different modes of knowledge. Achieving that interaction is knowledge management.

Nonaka has presented us with a model to help us better understand this interaction and its effects. This is the spiral of knowledge as illustrated below.

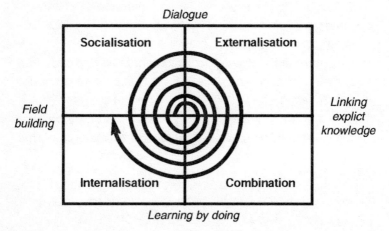

Each mode of knowledge needs to be converted into content so that it can be used by the organisation. For example, when we work on socialisation we produce what Nonaka calls *sympathised* knowledge: shared mental models of what should happen or shared technical skills of how something is done. In a like manner, externalisation creates *conceptual* knowledge, combination creates *systemic* knowledge and finally internalisation produces *operational* knowledge. The first stage in the spiral conversion can be expressed as follows:

Tacit knowledge *to* Explicit knowledge

	Tacit knowledge	Explicit knowledge
Tacit knowledge *from*	**Sympathised knowledge** (Socialisation)	**Conceptual knowledge** (Externalisation)
Explicit knowledge	**Operational knowledge** (Internalisation)	**Systemic knowledge** (Combination)

We shall return to this model with examples later in the book. This knowledge content will be used to trigger the creation of new asset value knowledge through organisational or people interaction. Nonaka represents this by another dimension of the spiral:

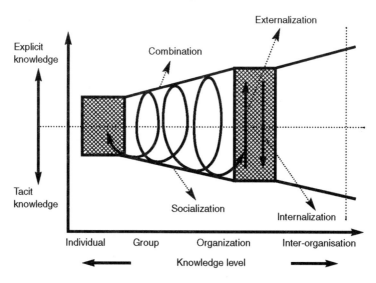

Summary

We have spent Sunday discovering the growing importance of knowledge as a key capital asset of any organisation. We further examined some of the theory that lies behind the concept of knowledge management and identified some clear benefits as:

- continuously improving existing products and services
- improving and extending core competencies
- developing new intellectual capital for the future.

On Monday we consider how to create an organisation that values and manages knowledge – the learning organisation.

Our work today can be summarised as:

- Recognising the growing power of knowledge in business and the need to manage this asset
- Increasing our understanding of what constitutes knowledge and the distinction between explicit and tacit knowledge
- Recognising the role of information technology and the even more important role of people in knowledge management
- Examining the theory behind knowledge management.

The learning organisation

On Sunday we emphasised the importance of the working environment for the successful management of knowledge. The ideal workplace culture has been called the learning organisation and is defined thus:

A learning organisation is skilled at acquiring, creating and transferring knowledge and at modifying its behaviour to reflect new knowledge and insights.

Today we will examine elements of this concept and highlight the principles, characteristics and activities of a learning organisation.

The learning organisation does not exist as a fact. It is a concept similar to total quality management or business process re-engineering. Like those concepts it *can* become a buzzword or a flavour of the month fad. On Tuesday we will discuss how to avoid such pitfalls. For now let's reflect on how Peter Senge, author of the *Fifth Discipline* and a leading proponent of learning organisations, described the concept. 'We are taking a stand for a vision, for creating the type of organisation's we would truly like to work within and which can thrive in a world of increasing interdependency and change.'

In his 'fieldbook', Senge stated that the core of a learning organisation is based on five learning disciplines:

The five learning disciplines – lifelong programs of study

1. *Personal mastery* – learning to expand our personal capacity to create the results we most desire, and creating an organisational environment which encourages all its members to develop themselves towards the goals and purposes they choose.
2. *Mental models* – reflecting upon, constantly clarifying, and improving our internal pictures of the world, and seeing how they shape our actions and decisions.
3. *Shared vision* – building a sense of commitment in a group, by developing shared images of the future we seek to create, and the principles and guiding practices by which we hope to get there.
4. *Team learning* – transforming conversational and collective thinking skills, so that groups of people can reliably develop intelligence and ability greater than the sum of individual members' talents.

5. *Systems thinking* – a way of thinking about, and a language for describing and understanding, the focus and interrelationships that shape the behaviour of systems. This discipline helps us to see how to change systems more effectively, and to act more in tune with the larger processes of the natural and economic world.

These disciplines are more than a program of study; they are techniques which need to be practised. Some people have an innate gift for a discipline; others will need extensive help and monitoring. This all sets a new perspective for company training and development programs.

It must already be clear that the learning organisation requires a people dominated strategy as opposed to an IT based strategy – a company direction that will build people's competencies and help them to share experiential knowledge. In other words organisations must *value* the ideas, intellect, experience and innovative skills of their people. This constitutes a dramatic change from the traditional division between thinkers and doers which still persists widely in business.

But people are not an academic abstract. They are real live human beings with a diversity of skills, experiences and attitudes. Within the organisation they already work at differing levels and have responsibilities not necessarily commensurate with their latent talents. There is no one, prescribed, organisational quick fix to manage this diversity. Each company has to work at its unique solution.

Technology, people and learning

The main reason for capturing knowledge is to enable it to be shared and thus trigger innovation. Technological advances in recent years, particularly the convergence of telecommunications and computing, allow knowledge to be more easily exchanged within and across corporations, regardless of geographical boundaries. Data-warehouses and the intranet allow staff to access corporate knowledge wherever they are. A consultant or salesperson for example, working anywhere in the world, can access a colleagues' shared expertise immediately.

Technology makes it possible to store and manipulate vast amounts of information, but knowledge management involves more than this. People are central to the formation and use of knowledge. If knowledge is to be shared and used, managers need to:

- design systems that fit *people's* needs
- provide continuous education, training and *mentoring* in systems use and in the benefits of knowledge sharing
- take account of potential behavioural problems, such as a reluctance to share knowledge or spend time on updating databases
- encourage and reward employees who positively commit to continuous learning.

The learning organisation and knowledge management both start as an attitude of mind and a new perspective of the changing business world. Nick Willard, in a perceptive article published in *Managing Information* (June 1999), linked both with an interesting visualisation of the people axis of Nonaka's spiral of knowledge. He first looks at the issues from an individual, team and organisational perspective.

Individual
The greater the knowledge acquired by the individual, the greater the creative potential of the organisation. Therefore, projects such as Open Learning, Corporate Libraries and Universities and other learning initiatives contribute to the growth of personal knowledge. Learning and creativity are two sides of the same coin. This will also impact on payment and contract terms.

On another level, how can the individual be helped and encouraged to articulate (in Nonaka's terms, *externalise*) their ideas? We will examine some specific tools in this area on Friday.

Team
In recent years there has been a focus on teamwork and there is now an emphasis on the structure and techniques for the conduct of team meetings to make them more effective. Teams must have a purpose or they are in danger of becoming just another meeting. Electronic systems such as video-conferencing, data warehouses, e-mail and intranet can merge expertise from around the world for learning purposes.

Organisation
Projects at this level tend to be of two types: those that are concerned with changing culture or working environment and those concerned with releasing and using knowledge. As we have seen, changing the culture is vital or little will happen. We start to look at that process on Tuesday.

Buckman Laboratories, a leader in the field of knowledge
management, achieved a strong customer focused culture
in introducing a Knowledge Information Centre, online
forums, virtual conferencing and corporate wide e-mail.
These all enabled individuals and teams to 'tap' the
knowledge of colleagues around the world as triggers to
develop their own knowledge.

The organisational role in releasing and using knowledge
means providing a database with a networking access,
usually now in intranet form. This enables people to ask
knowledge questions such as, *Who handles this? Who knows
about that? What are we doing in this area?*

This is a good moment to differentiate between information and knowledge:

- An information base refers to recorded knowledge contained in reports, documents, patents, specifications etc.
- A knowledge base is still explicit (or it cannot be recorded) but links people and work processes to the information.

An imaginative walk through the modes of knowledge in the spiral of knowledge will help illustrate these points:

1 An individual starts with the gem of an idea and manages to find a way to express it. The idea has now moved from tacit to explicit – *externalisation*.
2 The individual combines this idea with other ideas or known concepts to create knowledge content – *combination*.
3 The developed idea has now converted from explicit back to tacit – *socialisation*.
4 The idea is now articulated, made explicit and spread to more people and steadily the idea is combined to prevent a bigger idea and so on. This all involves further internalisation, externalisation and socialisation as represented in the diagram on the following page.

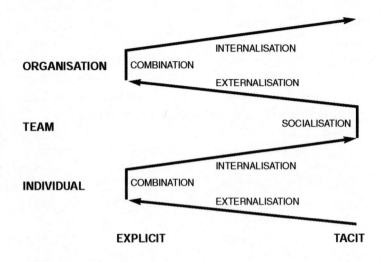

Nick Willard's version of the knowledge spiral

A new perspective

The last two decades have seen a transformation in management perspective. A participative style is replacing the authoritative mode. An influencing factor has been the obvious advance in its effects on technology and the knowledge worker. However, the dominating factor is the emergence of the global economy.

The rise of Japan as a major competitive force did more to create the global market than any other factor. Japan's success at penetrating complacent western markets led other nations to join the fray. Technology has helped the process move more quickly.

In the west, shaken executives looked for new ways of managing their enterprises. The quality revolution spawned

Total Quality Management (TQM) and its derivatives business process re-engineering, team work, customer care and others. The learning organisation and knowledge management are evolutionary developments of that response to the launch of the global economy. As we work through the week we will see similarities arising from this source.

The learning wheel

Charles Handy coined the term 'learning wheel' in his book *The Age of Unreason* in 1989 but the concept had been explored, in depth, by David Kolb in his 1984 book *Experimental Learning*. TQM adherents will also recognise its similarity to the 'Shewhart cycle' (*Plan, do, study, act*) promoted by Dr Deming.

People learn in a cyclical fashion. They pass between action and reflection, between activity and repose. To make effective change take place, managers need to find ways to link to the individual's cycle. The most effective tool is to use the learning wheel on an individual basis and ensure that teams are educated to use the same tool in their deliberations.

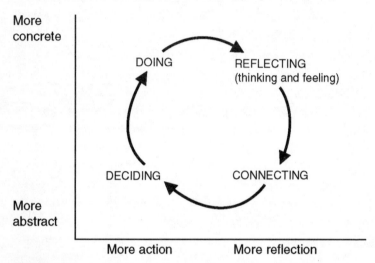

The learning wheel

The elements of the wheel can be used by individuals or a group of people to help develop an organised and disciplined way to learn from working experience. Knowledge from and about our work is developed as follows:

- *Reflection* – observing and thinking about what has happened. As a group exercise it could take the form of a post-mortem on a specific workplace action, asking questions and discussing such areas as what was done? How did it relate to our objectives or values? Could it have been done differently? How? This is a sharing of experiences on thinking and feeling about the process – what Senge calls *public reflection*.

- *Connecting* – creating ideas and possibilities for action. Using the knowledge gained from reflection to improve in the future.
- *Deciding* – selecting from or combining the ideas developed in the connecting stage to establish a method for acting. As a group this is joint or team planning.
- *Doing* – performing the task and then returning immediately to the reflection stage.

Key activities

We have noted that the learning organisation and knowledge management have evolved from the changes in management thinking brought about by the quality revolution. Five key activities in learning organisations provide the link from TQM and continuous improvement. They are:

- Systematic problem solving
- Experimentation
- Learning from past experience
- Learning from others
- Transferring knowledge

Systematic problem solving
All the tools used in problem solving, from a process diagram to cause and effect diagrams (see another book in this series, *Understanding Total Quality Management in a Week*, for a description of these tools), are in reality *learning tools*. A systematic approach will ensure that the knowledge gathered is codified, stored and made available for everyone.

Experimentation
People are encouraged to experiment with new approaches to their work and the tools they use. Driven by the concept of continuous improvement, experimentation is a major element in innovation. A learning cycle approach will once again ensure that the lessons learnt are available.

Learning from past experience
The organisation provides *time* for regular reviews of work processes, projects and practices. The important element here is to capture the tacit experiences from those involved and translate them into explicit knowledge for wider distribution.

Learning from others
The learning organisation is constantly benchmarking (see another book in this series, *Understanding Benchmarking in a Week*, for a full description of this process) the processes and practices throughout their own company and in other organisations. If the organisation is constantly reviewing

as above, then this activity is assisted. Benchmarking is a powerful knowledge provider and if adapted rather than adopted can also be a major stimulant to knowledge creation.

Transferring knowledge
Learning organisations do not allow knowledge to moulder away in 'Knowledge Warehouses' or are not even satisfied that everyone has access to the knowledge. They take an active rather than passive approach to transferring knowledge. Regular 'did you know' forums or intranet conferencing drive the process.

Summary

Today we have seen that the learning organisation is a cultural approach and management style that creates the environment for knowledge management. Specifically we learned that:

- The learning organisation is a concept
- There are five learning disciplines
- The learning organisation is a people dominated strategy which requires strong management support
- The tools of the knowledge spiral and the learning wheel are complementary
- Key activities are derived from TQM.

To an extent, both Sunday and Monday have been concerned with the theory behind knowledge management and the learning organisation. Tomorrow we switch to the practical aspects of making it happen.

Getting started

From all that we learned on Sunday and Monday, it must be clear that developing a knowledge creating organisation is not a short-term project. The process is going to take time, resources and eventually involve everyone in the organisation.

The process can be visualised as another phase in the never ending road to continuous improvement that started with TQM. Whether we are already on this road or are about to join it we need some important information to help us plan and prepare a roadmap for our journey. In other words we need to assess:

- Where does the journey start or where are we now?
- What is the destination or purpose of the journey?
- What problems are we likely to meet on the journey or what barriers are there to our progress?

Assessment

Far too many corporate initiatives are launched without sufficient pre-thought or real understanding of the need to change. As a result the progress is patchy and tends to fold when it meets the first real problem. That is the basis for the much maligned *'flavour of the month'* approach to executive launched initiatives.

Assessment is vital for this journey. We aim to develop an organisation based both on learning and maximising the potential of the company's knowledge. For the long term integrity of the process we should start as we mean to go on. We need to learn more about our own organisation and the possible barriers to change that we may meet on the journey. The assessment provides the knowledge that is needed to prepare an implementation plan. The plan itself will be the subject for Wednesday.

The importance of this initial assessment cannot be over emphasised. To date, many companies, particularly in the USA, have launched knowledge management initiatives without sufficient pause for thought and planning. They listen to the latest management guru or are persuaded by the leading IT consultants that they cannot waste a moment in launching the drive for knowledge management. Only later do they realise that the initiative has not quite delivered the competitive advantage they wanted.

The IT trap

The IT dominated approach to implementing knowledge management is a dangerous trap for the unwary starter. It is akin to building a school, equipping it with the best desks, chairs, blackboards and all the books needed, and then expecting to have a successful educational centre. We all know that is not enough. The equipment will certainly be a great help, and is therefore important, but real success can only come from the organised interaction between the human beings involved; teachers and pupils. All the best schools create an environment conducive to both learning and to establishing a shared commitment.

The establishment of a learning organisation dedicated to the management of knowledge should be seen in a similar light. Yes, the IT and systems framework is important but the real release of the potential of knowledge will come from a sharing and learning culture. As with the school it also requires leadership but we will return to that aspect later.

The consultant trap

Unfortunately many management consultants do take an IT dominated approach. That is why there are so many examples of companies who have made major investments in installing intranet, data warehouses, other IT tools and supporting software but seem no nearer the knowledge management objective than when they started.

In the field of knowledge management few consultants offer a holistic service that can provide a co-ordinated approach to both the IT and the culture issues. There is nothing wrong with employing more than one, even several consultants on the process but it will require co-ordination and a clear definition of the role of each. We can learn from the TQM era. Those who blindly followed the prescriptive approaches of gurus or consultants met relative failure. Those who used outside consultants to facilitate the organisation to plan for and implement their *own* unique solutions generally met with greater success.

From this it should be clear that calling in consultants, from however big or famous a stable, to implement knowledge management is to court disaster. First take some preparatory learning steps before diving in at the deep end. The preparatory steps are:

- A detailed assessment of where the organisation stands in relation to knowledge
- An assessment of the current culture or environment for change
- An assessment of the current IT position
- Defining a purpose or strategic statements on knowledge and competence requirements
- A holistic measure of the delta or the difference between where we are and where we want to be.

Each of these steps will require awareness sessions and the selection of internal facilitators. External consultants can also be valuable as they bring an outside perspective and specific knowledge; but only as advisors at this stage.

All these steps should be completed before developing an implementation plan. For the rest of today we will therefore concentrate on the assessment steps.

Locational assessment

Organisational culture and capabilities can differ widely
from location to location. The same breadth of variance will
often be found between differing disciplines, functions or
departments. Now add the diversity of national cultures in
an international company and we have a company
patchwork quilt. Of course this depends on the size and
complexity of the organisation but this divergence will be
an important factor in planning. For example, will the
change be implemented at the same pace across the whole
company?

Scale of the assessment

An early decision must be made about the scale of the
assessment. This will partly depend on the organisational
complexity we have noted but should also take account of
the following questions:

- Is this to be a corporate wide assessment including
  every international component?
- Even if corporate wide, are there some typical locations or
  operations that can safely be used as 'statistical samples'?
- If there is a phased approach are the locations defined?
- Is the assessment to encompass all levels? If not what
  are the levels?
- Do we have sufficient skills or do we need consultant
  help with the assessment?

Assessment techniques

There are a wide variety of techniques available ranging
from employee surveys to technical audits. They include
focus groups, individual in-depth interviews, brainstorming,
e-mail questions and others. They each have a purpose and

are designed to suit different situations. For example, in this case the cultural assessment is dealing with people's perceptions as well as facts and will require a technique designed to uncover tacit knowledge. Another case may involve an IT assessment which will require a technical audit collecting predominantly explicit knowledge, though there are some tacit areas relating to human interface.

Typical cultural assessment
A company location, facility or manufacturing plant gathers together the leading functional managers and key knowledge workers. The internal or external consultant leading the assessment process will then give an awareness presentation explaining the objectives and issues. Some *perception questionnaires* are then distributed for immediate completion (examples of typical perception questionnaires were illustrated in another book in this series, *Understanding Total Quality Management in a Week*).

The session closes with the distribution of some more questionnaires for completion later and the scheduling of individual interviews with all present. The individual interviews discuss the completed questionnaires and opinions or quotations are anonymous thus easing the communication.

The findings from all of these locational assessments can be amalgamated to provide a company wide assessment as well as individual statistics. The whole process also helps to increase understanding of the need for change and individual ownership of the process. As a result, assessment not only gathers the information for planning but it actually starts the process of change.

Knowledge assessment

The assessment is seeking information or answers to questions as to our current status. For example in the knowledge sector some typical questions are:

- What patents, copyrights or licences do we hold?
- What brands or other market advantages do we have?
- Which of our product, production or operational technologies or practices are key assets?
- What are our prime competencies?
- Which of our current alliances and associations bring additional knowledge or competence?
- How many of our products and services have remained fundamentally unchanged for $2\frac{1}{2}$ years or more?
- Which processes or practices have been adapted from the result of internal or external benchmarking over the last 5 years?
- What additional knowledge, competence or marketing opportunity have we gained from acquisitions over the last 5 years?
- What attempts have been made to date to visualise, measure and manage intellectual capital?

Thoroughgoing answers to these questions will immediately prompt further questions. These relate directly to the organisation's strategy for the future. That is the principal reason for investing in the concept of knowledge management. These questions can be summarised as:

1. What additional intellectual knowledge does the organisation need to support the strategy and achieve a sustained competitive advantage?

WHAT ARE YOUR ORGANISATION'S PRIME COMPETENCIES?

2. What elements of that knowledge could we acquire externally through new licences, alliances, acquisitions and benchmarking?
3. What elements of that knowledge could be created internally by the leverage of our current assets through a new knowledge management culture?

These questions relate directly to the organisational business strategy which we will return to in more depth on Wednesday.

Cultural assessment
The knowledge assessment is aimed at measuring the business status in relation to knowledge management. The other element is to assess the organisational environment or the degree to which the people and the systems are ready for the implementation of the new direction. The typical questions which need to be answered in this segment can be summarised as follows.

Cultural questions – does the organisation:

- communicate effectively at and between every level or function to delight the customer?
- have a sharing culture, in which there is a natural reaction to help colleagues?
- encourage knowledge creation or innovation through team structures?
- support constructive experiment and risk taking?
- have an education and training programme to encourage continuous learning?
- have management that provide the time and resources to take part in learning and sharing exercises?
- tolerate barriers to communication or sharing related to positional status, length of service, academic qualifications or perceived functional importance?
- make efforts to capture, define and codify experiential and tacit knowledge?
- communicate and exploit knowledge effectively?
- make knowledge easy to find?
- encourage internal and external benchmarking?
- have specific programmes to elicit knowledge from customers, suppliers and other associated external bodies?
- carry out in-depth interviews of both terminating and joining employees to elicit knowledge?
- reward or recognise individual and team knowledge sharing?

The other key area for assessment is the current status of the organisation's information and communications technology. We are going to consider the key requirements in that area on Thursday and so that will be the most appropriate section in which to consider the assessment issues in technology.

All of these assessments will provide vital knowledge to the planning team considering how to both implement a strategy to create a learning organisation and to manage knowledge effectively. In effect the assessment will help to define the barriers that have to be overcome for a successful implementation.

Typical barriers

There are always barriers to change. They are not necessarily indicative of previous bad management but may be the result of changing technology, products and industry or market practices. In today's global market, new cultures, competition and political action outside the control of the organisation may well create barriers to the easy implementation of the organisation's strategies.

Whatever the source or cause, these barriers must be identified and defined so that plans can be made to tackle the following broad areas of obstruction:

- Barriers to recognising the need
- Organisational barriers
- Informal cultural barriers
- Technological barriers.

We will consider each of them in turn.

Barriers to recognising the need

The greatest barrier to recognising the need to change is current success and complacency. There are several examples of large corporations being caught out by change of markets or evolution of technologies.

IBM and Xerox are recent examples of large corporations who failed to recognise or use knowledge available to them and paid a heavy price. IBM management were so seduced by the revenues from large computer dominated distributed networks that they failed to anticipate the pace of change in the personal computer (PC) environment. They were masters of PC technology but failed to invest in the supporting software and the change in market direction. As a result 60,000 loyal, knowledge intensive IBM employees had their contracts terminated.

For similar complacent reasons Xerox recognised far too late that Canon's new 'total cartridge' innovation was about to decimate the maintenance dominated copier market. Again loyal employees paid the price and the corporation was condemned to years of catch-up. Now both organisations show evidence of having learned the lesson. Both are also enthusiastic supporters of the knowledge management movement.

Many other organisations of varying size and in all sectors of endeavour find that current success can be a barrier to change. They are so busy that there is no time to keep up with changing management practices or emerging technologies. Perhaps more important, even when sections of the organisation closest to the market place *do* recognise changing circumstances they are not listened to. Perhaps in reality it is not so much that they are totally unaware of new knowledge but they do not have the time to devote the resources needed to comprehend the significance to their own operations of these new potentials. They do not take ownership of the need to change.

Organisational barriers
The structures and formal procedures of the organisation may suit the current environment but create barriers to change towards a *different environment* as follows:

- Organisational structure designed on a hierarchical, matrix or project orientation
- Communication channels
- Internal charging and measurement procedures
- Command and control procedures
- Contracts of employment
- Recognition and reward systems
- External financial, political and industry associations
- International and business autonomy
- Procedures for setting objectives, responsibilities and co-operation.

Informal cultural barriers
Many informal barriers emanate from the organisational barriers. They come about from people's *perceptions* of what is

expected or what seems the personal route to success, such as:

- Perception of values built-up from experience
- Leadership versus management
- Fear of making a mistake or the power of knowledge
- Lack of trust
- Time pressures, real or imagined
- Personal empowerment
- Personal history or experiential knowledge.

Technological barriers
We have already noted that we will deal with key issues arising from technology on Thursday but there are two issues which are pertinent to these discussions.

1. Is the organisation committed to achieving a learning and knowledge management culture though technology or aiming for a more gradual people based change? Both are valid approaches but the choice could depend upon the IT literacy of the organisation. This is an area for assessment. A non IT-literate work force will ignore or totally misuse a massive investment in technology. The gradual introduction of technology coupled with intensive development and training in both sharing and IT skills could be the right approach in this environment. Equally, a failure to upgrade technology in an IT skilled environment will have an impact on morale and utilisation.
2. The current performance of existing technology and its management are also crucial issues in the assessment of technology. A series of issues such as reactivity to user need, reliability, flexibility and perceived awareness of the issues arising from knowledge management are areas for audit.

Summary

Today we have started the journey towards a knowledge based culture by making a detailed assessment of the organisation's current status and defining the key barriers to success. We have recognised the value of taking time for thought and assessment so as not to fall in to the quick fix trap and the associated dangers of being dominated by IT or consultants. We have started the process of finding the best solution for this unique organisation.

We have considered the following areas in detail:

- The scale of the involvement and of the process
- Some assessment techniques
- How to make a knowledge assessment
- The issues of cultural and organisational assessment
- The typical barriers to success.

On Wednesday we will use these assessments to help prepare the strategies and plan the actions needed to implement knowledge management successfully.

Planning for success

Achieving success with knowledge management is not easy
and will not happen by accident. Nor will it happen as a
natural consequence of investing in the latest information
technology system. Success requires focussed thought and
planning before leaping into implementation action mode.

There are three distinct elements in the planning process.
They are the subject for Wednesday and they can be
summarised as:

- Defining the organisation's strategy for knowledge
  management
- Selecting a team to prepare the plan and to later
  act as change agents or facilitators in the initial
  implementation phase
- Preparing the action plan for implementation —
  the plan will include schedules, definition of resources
  required and the measures for success.

Knowledge management strategy

Any organisation that depends on highly skilled people
and the development of ideas should have a knowledge
management strategy. But the way they leverage these
skills and ideas may determine the strategic direction and
mode of implementation.

Some companies will choose to automate knowledge management while others will emphasise a people centred, knowledge sharing approach. Both are valid approaches and the choice should be determined by the nature of the organisation and its business strategy. Choosing the wrong approach or trying to implement both processes at the same time can be dangerous.

Before considering these alternatives we should clarify the difference between the business strategy for the content of knowledge and the strategy for implementing knowledge management. On Tuesday we noted the organisation's prime competencies and knowledge content as part of the assessment. That information was to support the business strategy. Today we are concentrating on the strategy or process for sharing and managing knowledge, rather than on its content.

An article in the *Harvard Business Review* on knowledge management (Morten T. Hansen, Nitin Nohria and Thomas Tierney, March 1999) described research into how different consultant companies approached the subject. They described the alternative knowledge management approaches as a choice between the *codification* and the *personalisation* strategies.

- The codification strategy is centred on computer systems. Knowledge is documented, codified and stored in databases (knowledge warehouses) where it can be accessed and used easily by anyone in the organisation.
- The personalisation strategy is centred on people with in-depth knowledge, which they have developed from experience and study, and is mainly shared through direct person-to-person contact. Here the computer is used to help people communicate knowledge rather than to store it.

The article notes that though examples are based on consulting companies they are not unique to consulting. The two strategies are at work in many other sectors. Indeed the choice between codification and personalisation is the central issue facing all organisations involved in knowledge management. This is a decision for the executives of the company and is closely related to the nature of the organisation and its business objectives.

The diagram opposite, based on the Harvard study, shows how competing consulting firms organise their knowledge management.

How Consulting Firms Manage Their Knowledge

Codification

Provide high-quality, reliable and fast information systems implementation by reusing codified knowledge.

Reuse Economics:

- Invest once in a knowledge asset; reuse it many times
- Use large teams with a high ratio of associates to partners
- Focus on generating large overall revenues

People-to-documents

- Develop an electronic document system that codifies, stores, disseminates, and allows reuse of knowledge
- Invest heavily in IT; the goal is to connect people with reusable codified knowledge
- Hire new college graduates who are well suited to the reuse of knowledge and the implementation of solutions
- Train people in groups and through computer-based distance learning
- Reward people for using and contributing to document databases

Personalisation

Provide creative, analytically rigorous advice on high-level strategic problems by channelling individual expertise.

Expert Economics:

- Charge high fees for highly customised solutions to unique problems
- Use small teams with a low ratio of associates to partners
- Focus on maintaining high profit margins

Person-to-person

- Develop networks for linking people so that tacit knowledge can be shared
- Invest moderately in IT; the goal is to facilitate conversations and the exchange of tacit knowledge
- Hire M.B.A.s who like problem solving and can tolerate ambiguity
- Train people through one-on-one mentoring
- Reward people for directly sharing knowledge with others

Andersen Consulting,
Ernst & Young

McKinsey & Company,
Bain & Company

A close look at the previous diagram provides some guidance on the selection of the alternative strategies. The codification route lends itself to organisations that rely heavily on explicit knowledge. The personalisation strategy is more directed at companies that have a high reliance on tacit knowledge. Some other characteristics may provide guidance:

Favours codification	*Favours personalisation*
• Similar products or services for each customer	• One off products, services or projects for each customer
• Work may demand high skills but relatively little creativity	• High premium on creativity and innovation
• Business and market strategies based on analysis of specific knowledge	• Business and market strategies based on 'feel' or intuition
• Ratio of operational staff to leaders very high	• Ratio of operational staff to leaders almost non-existent
• Relative similarity in operating characteristics over locations and functions	• High diversity in operating characteristics over locations, functions and markets

These characteristics can only be simplistic guidelines so the decision must be based on *real* knowledge of the organisation. There are two other elements which must be taken into consideration in making the strategic decision. One relates to the assessments we considered on Tuesday. The other recognises the possibility of differing approaches in specific sectors of the organisation.

If the assessments indicated that the operational environment is not suitable for knowledge management the organisation must now look at long-term phased implementation. The IT systems may need a total replacement or upgrading, resulting in delay and high cost. The cultural assessment may have indicated that employees' current perceptions would be a major barrier to introducing a sharing environment. This situation could require long-term involvement in education and training and a major transformation in both management personnel and personnel policies. These factors demand a phased implementation of the selected strategy.

In many organisations, functional areas such as research and development, product design and other specialist innovative areas may exhibit distinct and different environments to the rest of the organisation. All of these characteristics will influence the strategy for implementing knowledge management.

Selecting a team

In reality the team may have been selected before the assessment phase and members of the teams may have taken part in leading the assessment. However, the team must be selected to prepare the actual plan for introducing knowledge management.

In selecting a team we have two considerations: the purpose of the team and the composition of the team. Let's look at each in turn.

Purpose of the team
Let's be clear from the start. The purpose of the team is *not* to manage knowledge. That is the purpose of the management and people working together to achieve the organisation's objectives. The purpose of the team is to plan for and launch the *change* from the current operational mode to one based on knowledge management. Effectively this is a 'change management' team. This is another lesson we can learn from prior experience in launching TQM and like initiatives.

Unfortunately many organisations have made this mistake. They have fallen into the temptation of forming specialised departments, e.g. 'the knowledge creation department', and appointments, e.g. 'futurist-in-chief'. This is all bureaucratic nonsense and only results in new empires which only succeed in obscuring the issues. If any reader doubts this strong warning look at the following individual or team titles found in an examination of knowledge management literature:

- Director of innovation
- Director of knowledge mobilisation
- Director of competitive learning
- Vice President of Learning
- Director of intelligence
- Leader, learning and change
- Chief knowledge officer
- Corporate Director of Intellectual Capital
- Transformation Officer
- Intellectual Asset Appraiser
- Competence Leader
- Process Competency Knowledge Management Analyst
- Learning person
- Director of Asset Reuse

A sceptic might suggest that the BBC script team for 'Yes Minister' would be hard pressed to find a more expansive list of bureaucratic titles.

The strategic objective of the corporation is to maximise the knowledge assets arising from the operators of the business. In other words, knowledge management should become 'the way we work around here'. It is not a new function requiring a new department. The purpose of the team is to facilitate the change from the present environment to one based on knowledge management.

The team must recognise that it is part of its function to plan its own elimination.

Selection of the team
The members of this team are being selected to plan the process of change and then to act as the initial change agents or facilitators to help introduce knowledge management across the organisation. They are not being chosen to manage knowledge on behalf of the organisation. That can only be done by managers and people in their normal roles. As we will see on Friday, further teams may need to be established to manage elements of the process as it develops.

The composition of the team will be dependent on the size and maturity of the organisation in relation to knowledge management and information technology. A further influence is the geographic dispersal of the organisation.

The team should represent all the key functional areas of the organisation's operations, e.g. marketing, design, production, delivery, service, personnel, IT and finance. Within these broad boundaries the geographic locations should be represented.

Specialist knowledge of IT networking and some long-term service experience of the organisation at a senior level are vital for the team to operate effectively. Additionally, knowledge of the behavioural sciences can be of help. With the possible exception of the team leader these are not necessarily full-time or permanent positions. They should all be operating at senior management/operational levels and the appointments could be viewed as short term secondments to a special task force. Generally, the team members should be selected from within the organisation. However, if there are no staff with codification and IT skills they will need to be recruited externally but this could be a source of delay.

All the same, the external viewpoint *can* bring a new perspective to the organisation. For this reason it is wise to seek experienced consultant help. They would act as facilitating aids to the team. It would be unwise to wholly rely on outside consultants to replace any lack of specialist skills. It could make the whole operation hostage to fortune.

Codification will be a new skill set to many organisations though it is key to the capturing and communication of knowledge. It is worth noting here that there is only one profession with specific training in this area – a qualified librarian. Until recently this has been a much under-valued profession. The early recruitment of a qualified librarian to play a senior role in the knowledge management initiative should be a priority.

The planning team should report to the chief executive officer through the team leader. As we have already noted, there are a growing number of titles for this post ranging from Vice President Knowledge Management to Knowledge Director. In the United States the favourite title seems to be settling around Chief Knowledge Officer (CKO) but they usually do see things in terms of Chiefs and Indians!

Chief Knowledge Officer

This is an extremely important post. The role is to provide the focus for the executive committee on the successful drive to implement the knowledge management initiative. Though the role clearly extends beyond just co-ordination it should not herald the establishment of a new functional empire. The CKO may need a small specialist team of internal consultants but the direction of the initiative should be through the operational directors and managers. In that sense the CKO is the knowledge management champion.

The post-holder will oversee and drive the business processes, infrastructure, culture change and information resource development which will allow quality knowledge to be captured in order to facilitate a sustained competitive advantage.

Knowledge management plan

The implementation of knowledge management is one of the biggest internal projects the organisation will experience. It will ultimately change the working environment and experience of every employee and it will almost certainly require substantial resources. For these reasons the process must be carefully planned.

The plan must therefore provide:

- Specific management direction and goals for results
- Detailed implementation activities to support systematic technical and organisational change
- Details of the timeframe and resources required.

Components of the plan

To meet the plan objectives we will need to define the following plan components and actions:

- Strategy, principles and values for the initiative
- Management structure and recruitment for change
- Education and training for every employee
- IT systems and other tools to support the process
- Key opportunities and priorities for knowledge capture and creation
- Implementation launch and actions
- Goals and criteria for success for both the technological and the culture change, including regular auditing
- Timetable and resources required.

We discussed the strategy for knowledge management earlier today but it still has to be spelled out and shared with all employees as part of the launch of the initiative. The timetable and financial resources needed are specific to each plan so are not part of our consideration. The other components of the plan will be covered over the next three days.

Summary

Today we have covered the elements involved in preparing to launch a knowledge management initiative. We have recognised the scale of the process of change and therefore the importance of planning. It is going to be a long journey so we need a roadmap – that is the plan.

In summary we covered:

- The issues involved in establishing a strategy
- The alternative between a codification or personalisation approach
- The establishment and selection of a planning team
- The post of Chief Knowledge Officer
- The importance of IT and Library skills
- The plan and its components.

Tomorrow, we look at the systems component of the plan.

Systems support

Support for the process of knowledge management has both *hard* and *soft* elements. The purpose of the hard systems is to enable the developing knowledge to be stored and transported so that it can be shared. The purpose of the soft systems is to modify the traditional culture systems so that all in the organisation *learn to learn* and want to share knowledge for the benefit of all.

Hard systems

It is not the purpose of this book to provide a detailed analysis of computer systems for knowledge management. The variety available and the pace of new technology developments would make the book out of date before it was published. However, those systems elements that we should consider together with guidelines for software application systems are as follows:

- Intranet
- Data warehouses
- Communications developments
- Guidelines for application software.

Soft systems

As we saw earlier in the week, a major element in the success or failure of knowledge management is the degree to which a sharing culture can be established.

Obviously much of this culture relates to the attitudes of individuals but there are systems and tools that can support the culture change. The organisation can also take strategic decisions to support the creation of new knowledge. The soft systems and strategies can be summarised as:

- Education and training
- Knowledge collection tools
- Benchmarking
- Strategic alliances.

For the rest of Thursday we will consider each of these hard and soft systems in detail. Some of the managerial elements of supporting the change will be covered on Friday.

Intranet

An intranet is an internal network which can be likened to a dedicated internet for an organisation. British Telecom (BT), with over 80,000 dedicated users, consider their own intranet to be the company's central nervous system. They see it as the core of their operations and claim that it has yielded phenomenal business benefits both in terms of cost savings and cultural change.

An intranet acts as a corporate wide, personnel directory providing address, phone numbers and organisational role in the company, as well as their whereabouts, responsibilities, skill sets and process experience. The directory can provide direct (or 'click') access to process knowledge through individual and process websites. If desired the intranet can be organised to provide extranet communication with customers, suppliers and other 'knowledge sites'.

BT also defined four key stages in the introduction of its intranet – each one of which is closely linked to both adding value to the operations and financial benefits that have accrued:

1. The publication of information electronically, creating identifiable cost savings.
2. The interaction between the user and the intranet to source knowledge, change work methods and improve productivity.
3. Transaction via automated processes, reducing 'paper pushing' and administration.
4. Collaboration and knowledge sharing among partners, suppliers and customers to provide new knowledge and spark innovation.

Data warehouses

The massive increase in the computerisation of information in the early 1980s led to the development of software systems to organise these vast dumps of information into a corporate asset. The development of specialised data warehouses is now a major service industry. The characteristics of a data warehouse can be summarised thus:

- A data warehouse causes data to be integrated across the organisation, facilitating the search for discreet sets of information from all over the system
- It creates historical patterns which can help in future planning
- The data warehouse offers a combination of both detailed and summarised knowledge
- It encourages the codification of knowledge
- It encourages the asking of questions.

Communications developments

There are a number of new telecommunication
developments that are being or soon will be introduced.
They are likely to have a major impact on corporate
networks and substantially broaden the opportunities for
knowledge acquisition.

Developments in communications technology such as
optical fibre networks, gigabit ethernet and switching will
relieve congestion problems, increase capacity and
dramatically reduce the price of communications globally.

The focus on electronic commerce through the internet is
fostering a number of technical developments which will
provide high bandwidth communication between home
and business. Apart from improved capacity and speed at
reduced cost it will also provide secure connections.
Security is becoming an issue for business as knowledge is
increasingly seen as a financial asset.

A series of new satellite communications networks are now
coming into service providing voice, data, fax and paging
telephone services to global business travellers. This has
attracted substantial investment in the development of
'handsets', with direct communication achievable through a
'local satellite' overhead.

Application software

A significant proportion of the investment in knowledge
management is devoted to application software. The
following checklist of attributes forms the guidelines for
determining the usefulness of application software in the

knowledge management process. They are organised into three application steps:

1. Collection and codification
- *Codification* – allows screen icons for *depositing text* and applying it directly to specific knowledge projects
- *Recall* – attributes findings to *original sources* regardless of the current situation
- *Free form capability* – allows total content requirements to be met regardless of document length and format
- *Search editor* – robust search commands that impose rigorous interrogation of the database contents.

2. Synthesis
- *Thought sequencing* – graphical interaction between report conclusions and supporting evidence
- *Pattern recognition* – identifies recurrent patterns found in multiple sources
- *Update* – revises volatile information and changes in network with the ability to merge as required.

3. Presentation
- *Content integration* – sends reports throughout the network with the ability to merge as required
- *Annotation* – ensures personal notes, embedded queries and document pointers are maintained to allow personal contact
- *Directories* – shows content in outline form for easy navigation to knowledge areas
- *Content validation* – a controlled 'content gate' to filter unwanted data.

Software suppliers or programming consultants should meet the detailed standards described above.

Education and training

The most powerful vehicle available to achieve the cultural
change defined in the plan is education and training. There
is a difference between the two elements. For example, we
may agree that our children need sex education but there
would not be the same measure of agreement that they also
need practical sex training. In business we use education to
influence people's attitudes or mind set so that they take
common ownership of the need to change and seek to share
knowledge. We need training to learn communication and
knowledge management skills and tools. Some selected
people will also need to know how to manage change.

Education and training is therefore the fulcrum in
implementing knowledge management. A combination of
the assessment and the strategy will determine the general
content and degree of education and training required.
However, there are some further questions that should
have been answered at the planning stage:

- Will everyone in the organisation require the same
  provision?
- Does every employee have the same role in the
  knowledge management process?
- If you decide that the executives, managers, specialists
  and workers have different roles, how would you divide
  their educational needs?
- Would the standard knowledge management courses
  available achieve change in our organisation?

Finally, adult learning in business is most effective when it
directly relates to the workplace. Employees at all levels are

more likely to understand and retain knowledge if they
have an easy transition with practice of the new concept
and then an immediate opportunity to apply the concept to
their own work.

Knowledge collection tools

Knowledge management has come about because of the
growing recognition of the value of the knowledge held by
organisations. This asset is now called intellectual capital
and rivals the traditional capital assets. But this knowledge
has little value if it remains latent and is not used to
improve products and services or to create new knowledge.
So collecting the available knowledge and making it
available to be used by all of those who can make best use
of it in the organisation is the objective of knowledge
management.

The collection and codification of explicit knowledge needs
organisation and the technology support we have
discussed, but is *relatively* straightforward. Capturing tacit
knowledge is a very different matter and requires sustained
effort, cultural change and tools. In essence, tacit
knowledge is held within human brains rather than
computers. It is based on an internal combination of taught
skills and experience of *how it really works.* Many people
already see that knowledge (without expressing the
motivation) as their *personal asset* and the basis for their
future employment. As the emphasis on intellectual capital
grows, more individuals will calculate the value of their
tacit knowledge. This concept will be developed further on
Saturday but once again the importance of culture change
should be emphasised.

We will discuss some of the managerial approaches to this issue, such as 'knowledge crews' and 'knowledge pools', tomorrow. Today we will go on to consider some tools currently used to collect explicit knowledge to show how they can be utilised to capture tacit knowledge.

There is one other aspect of knowledge to consider: the sheer amount of knowledge available. Several organisations who have invested in knowledge management systems have found that the sheer avalanche of information has caused indigestion. So the first priority is to establish priorities for knowledge capture. The key to that decision is *process focus*. Identify the key business processes that are essential to delighting customers and you have found the key areas from which we can capture knowledge to our advantage.

There are a number of tools that were developed for the earlier era of total quality management and continuous improvement. Most of the improvement and problem solving tools can be used to collect data and, more importantly, could be used in interview or team discussion mode to liberate tacit knowledge. The most useful are process flow models and the process diagram.

The process flow model is to some extent related to knowledge map charting which we will touch on during Friday. The process diagram was originally designed to show the relationship of customers and suppliers to the process and perhaps more important, to establish the process requirements. At that stage the diagram was used to spell out the state of the process in explicit knowledge terms to aid process involvement. Each of the boxes in the diagram on the following page (used in continuous improvement for explicit knowledge) could also be used in one-to-one interviews or team discussions to develop the tacit experimental knowledge hidden in the process.

The power of this approach is that the completed explicit and tacit process diagrams are immediately linked by their process codification.

Study of this diagram, which relates to a hospital service issue, indicates its value as a tool to capture tacit knowledge. Each unit of the diagram can be discussed to find out what really happens. Questioning about real performance and difficulty faced in making the process work every time provides real knowledge for improvement. This is one example of developing standard templates for recording and accessing knowledge.

Acute Services Unit
Activity Analysis Diagram

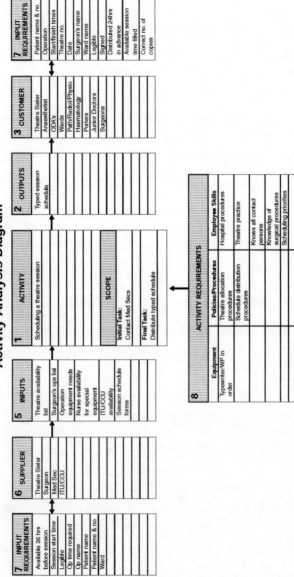

7 INPUT REQUIREMENTS
Available 36 hrs before session
Session start time
Legible
Op time required
Op name
Patient name
Patient name & no.
Ward

6 SUPPLIER
Theatre Sister
Surgeon
Med Sec
ITU/CCU

5 INPUTS
Theatre availability list
Surgeon's ops list
Operation equipment needs
Nurse availability for special equipment
ITU/CCU availability
Session schedule forms

1 ACTIVITY
Scheduling a theatre session
SCOPE
Initial Task: Contact Med Secs
Final Task: Distribute typed schedule

2 OUTPUTS
Typed session schedule

3 CUSTOMER
Theatre Sister
Anaesthetist
ODA's
Wards
Path/Radiol/Physio
Haematology
Porters
Junior Doctors
Surgeons

7 INPUT REQUIREMENTS
Patient name & no.
Operation
Start/finish times
Theatre no.
Date
Surgeon's name
Ward name
Legible
Signed
Distributed 24hrs in advance
Available session time filled
Correct no. of copies

8 ACTIVITY REQUIREMENTS			
Equipment	Policies/Procedures	Employee Skills	
Typewriter/WP in order	Theatre allocation procedures	Hospital procedures	
	Schedule distribution procedures	Theatre practice	
		Knows all contact persons	
		Knowledge of surgical procedures	
		Scheduling priorities	

The familiar problem solving 'fishbone' diagram is another powerful questioning tool to 'free' tacit knowledge from the operation of a work process.

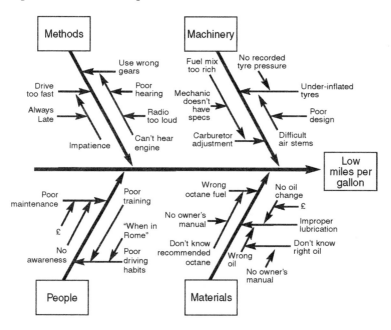

Benchmarking

Though a traditional management practice, 'benchmarking' became fashionable in Western business during the eighties. The process has been defined as:

The process of identifying, understanding and adopting outstanding practices and procedures from organisations anywhere in the world in order to help your own organisation improve its performance.

A moment's thought shows that it is also a reasonable description for collecting external knowledge or even internal knowledge from other areas of the organisation.

The emphasis on information technology has probably led to benchmarking and knowledge management not being linked in the business literature. The process of benchmarking is well organised and disciplined on an international basis (for more information on benchmarking see a book in this series entitled *Understanding Benchmarking in a Week*) and only needs links to the knowledge collection and codification systems of our organisation to provide powerful support for the knowledge management initiative.

Strategic alliances

The old adage, 'the more we know, the more we realise what we do not know' is particularly apt with knowledge management. The focus on knowledge as an asset helps identify missing pieces in our strategic jigsaw puzzle. As the organisation's awareness of its own knowledge assets grows, so it recognises that some areas are missing or that additional knowledge could provide new markets or lever existing knowledge to advantage. A high customer focus is a driver in this area.

A company strategy for acquisition or the establishment of strategic alliances and partnerships is a close parallel to the knowledge management strategy. Indeed, few corporations can now operate on a global scale without such alliances. Alliances are generally formed with other companies because of their specific market sector knowledge or specialist skills and products. Clearly such a strategy will be assisted if the organisation maintains a knowledge base on a wide variety of knowledge-based businesses. This is particularly relevant to new technology start-ups.

Partnerships

There are other opportunities to expand the knowledge asset and to trigger new knowledge creation. They can come from 'partnerships of trust' with external bodies which are not really business alliances. In many cases they become 'benchmarking' partners, sharing experience of best practices in both technology and processes. Typical arenas for such partnerships are:

- Suppliers – they are already in a partnership of common interest and can help each other; this also leads to single sourcing policies.
- Universities and other centres of excellence – they can be powerful knowledge creators in their own right and can help in the development of the organisation's people.

Summary

Today we have examined the systems and processes that will directly support the introduction of knowledge management. We noted that these can be divided into hard and soft systems. In particular we noted that neither set of systems would be effective unless the working environment was conducive to change. We therefore put a strong emphasis on education and training and the adaptation of familiar tools to assist the process.

Tomorrow we turn to the managerial and process elements of knowledge management.

Managing knowledge

Successful business leadership requires that we anticipate the future; we anticipate the future by understanding the present and managing that knowledge. Managing knowledge is a challenging task because it is hard to identify, and even more difficult to value and deploy to give the organisation a competitive edge in the market place. Additionally knowledge is never static – it is continuously changing and evolving.

Professor Sournitra Dutta of the European Institute of Business Administration (INSEAD) has stated the challenge and provided a useful classification of an organisation's assets in a 1997 article. His classifications are as follows:

- *Individual* – the individual knowledge worker is the fundamental unit for knowledge creation, storage and use within the organisation.

- *Group* – networks, both formal and informal, are usually an intangible but important knowledge asset within a company. Groups of individuals with shared experience often represent a cumulative body of knowledge.
- *Organisational* – the entire organisation can be viewed as embodying the result of a certain cumulative body of knowledge.
- *Knowledge links* – every company develops links with other firms (such as suppliers and customers) to exchange knowledge.

This model recognises that there are different *levels* of knowledge within an organisation. The culture tends to establish which level takes precedence in an organisation.

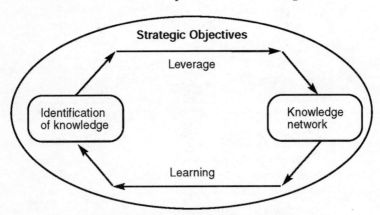

The strategic management of knowledge

The professor's diagram above reflects the essential components of the process of strategically managing knowledge. A company has to identify its knowledge network and learn from experience. All of this has to be done within the strategic objectives of the company.

This simple model contains the three major aspects of knowledge management:

- Storage
- Transfer
- Transformation

Identification of knowledge

Identification of assets at each level of knowledge is difficult. Individual expertise is not restricted to professionals or to top management. With individuals it may also be difficult to differentiate between real knowledge holding or access to other knowledge. Groups are not easy to identify let alone their group knowledge, and there are similar problems with organisational knowledge.

Knowledge has to be identified and codified if it is going to be leveraged within the knowledge network. The leverage is what helps companies to design better products, reduce time to market, be more competitive and delight the customers.

Process focus
The most important element in assisting knowledge identification is a strong focus on the business processes of the organisation. This needs to be tempered by a similar focus on customers to help determine priorities. We need to remember that in the main we are not seeking abstract knowledge as to how, for example, Henry VIII managed all his wives. We want to identify knowledge related to our business. Our business is wholly concentrated in its work processes.

Management must start by identifying the key processes, 'flow chart' them and start the identification of knowledge at each node of the flow. This also provides a *knowledge flow map* for each process rather than function or department. The process diagram we noted on Thursday is a tool to help this identification.

Pools of knowledge

It is important to move into knowledge management in a phased manner. The *big bang* approach creates confusion, indigestion or information overload. Give a manager one report and he may read it, give him twenty, and he is likely to bin them all. The process and knowledge flow will indicate groups of nodes which are critical. These can be considered as 'pools of knowledge' and expertise that are critical to corporate success. Concentrating on the process selection of pools of knowledge has an important cultural advantage over the alternative method of identifying

people pools of expertise. The people approach can over-emphasise the individual power of knowledge and thus inhibit the sharing process. A group of experts coming together as a team around a process objective will be much freer in sharing the vitally important tacit knowledge.

Launching the initiative

The action schedule for launching knowledge management will have been influenced by the assessment and spelled out in the plan. These actions will be both generic, covering all employees, and specific, through *'knowledge crews'*.

Generic activities

- Ensure that all employees are convinced of top management commitment to knowledge management through practical examples, e.g. e-mail messages, discussion groups and full participation in the education and training programme.
- Encourage the development of best practices with specialists, supported by intranet practice discussion groups.
- Make individuals responsible for the formation and continuous updating of all intranet directories, showing up-to-date titles, roles, skills and experience – this includes *every* level in the organisation. This will help the analysis of knowledge gaps in the workforce.
- Ensure that all induction and training programmes support co-operation and internal networking.
- Ensure that there is a continuous reference to the organisation's values and operating principles to help develop the sharing culture.

Pool activities

Small cross-functional teams are established for each pool of knowledge selected on a priority basis of asset value and in particular those that will yield quick and measurable returns. A key requirement is that members of the team have specific up-to-date process knowledge. The team activities can be summarised thus:

- Start by identifying the barriers to utilisation – IT weaknesses, incompatible systems, internal politics, departmental or national boundaries, incentive schemes and cultural issues.

- Consider appropriate knowledge management action – improving acquisition and search facilities, upgrading IT facilities (in co-ordination with the IT team), additional education or training needs and job rotation.
- Identify *owners* of the pool, provide appropriate training and define their responsibilities.
- Publicise through the intranet the pools and owners on the *knowledge map*.
- Identify any weak links between pools.
- Identify the knowledge in the pool using standard formats and communicate with the *codification team* ready for transport to the network.

Codification team

The purpose of this team is to set the standards for codification and indexing and then to ensure that all entries to the network are suitably coded. This is absolutely vital for the efficient storage and accessibility of knowledge to all interested parties. This is predominantly a librarian's skill rather than that of the IT specialist.

To some extent this team also acts as a 'gateway' to the network and has a part to play in filtering excess knowledge. Warehouses can become 'sink holes' of useless data and get bypassed because they are not of real value.

IT team

IT specialists will have a part to play in all teams but this team provides essential co-ordination. The crucial role of this team is to make sure that the IT systems are integrated into the knowledge management system. They will take the lead in selecting IT systems that support knowledge exchange in interactive communities throughout the organisation. They must take informed decisions about technological solutions that fit into the organisation's strategic direction. This team should be viewed as a strategic guiding force and will include non-IT specialists. It should not be formed by the current IT department though they should be represented.

Valuation team

It is advisable from the outset to set up a valuation team to establish standards and measurements for the valuation of the knowledge database. After all, valuation of intellectual capital is a prime objective of the process.

This element of accountancy is at its infancy and many accountants, for good reason, feel uncomfortable about the area of intangible assets as a contribution to the company's balance sheet. The opportunity for fraudulent misrepresentation is obvious. Valuation teams can develop acceptable measures and then apply them to defined 'knowledge packages' and help remove this accountant scepticism. This team requires a combination of accounting and process skills. (A new book entitled *Intellectual Capital* by Roos, Roos, Dragonetti and Edvinsson provides a thorough background to this whole area.)

Launching the intranet

Having completed the groundwork, the organisation's intranet should now be primed and ready for launch. However, a final precautionary review should be

undertaken. Indeed, BT's experience in launching their
intranet has highlighted a number of key factors which
other organisations would be well advised to consider
during the early stages of adopting an intranet system:

- All aspects of the business must be involved from the
  start, so that the intranet will respond to all requirements.
- Employee viewpoints must be sought and users should
  be encouraged to change the whole way they work, so
  that they can rely on the intranet for all the information
  they need.
- Look for an important announcement that can be
  released over the intranet to establish in everyone's mind
  the importance of the system, thus quelling early fears.
- Recognise that the intranet empowers people and will
  assist the process of cultural change as people begin to
  use the net pro-actively to promote their own ideas.
- Set appropriate boundaries and filters for information so
  as to prevent the loss of creativity or the multiplication of
  useless information.
- Be prepared for fast growth in use of the system after a
  fairly short introductory period. Users will become very
  frustrated with long waits or unavailability of information.
- Support the launch with the necessary training and
  support so that staff use is 'made easy'.

Summary

Today we concentrated on the management actions needed to implement knowledge management. In detail we looked at the:

- Levels of knowledge
- Strategic management of knowledge
- Identification of knowledge
- Knowledge network
- Process and customer focus
- Generic and specific actions involved in the launch.

Tomorrow we will consider the impact of this change on the individual.

Impact on the individual

Full circle

In many respects the modern knowledge worker can be compared with the medieval craftsman or mason.
He was a skilled professional with his own tools, free from the control of the local guilds (professional institutions or unions and conventional wisdom), living by his knowledge. He moved from site to site (a castle or cathedral) deriving his sense of worth and marketability by the demonstrable value of his work. His skills were developed through experience, working initially as an apprentice. His knowledge was totally tacit and passed on as received to another apprentice. Taking the analogy further, his knowledge manager was the priest.

There are certain differences (apart from not automatically being masculine) which cause some of the problems with modern day knowledge management. The modern knowledge worker is now separated from the actual process and the end results of their skills. Also the knowledge to be passed on is now embedded with either staff or line functions as well as equipment and software.

Returning to the similarities, the sense of freedom and independence is growing. Knowledge workers are sensing their individual value and are not prepared to endure the procedures and bureaucracy of the command and control business culture. The division between the thinkers and the doers of traditional business is clearly obsolete. The successful organisations of the future, based on the principles of knowledge management and the learning organisation, will be those who master the rising expectations of men and women employees; the ones that release their full potential. The new principles will be based on teamwork, sharing, creativity and continuous learning.

Motivating knowledge workers

Mahen Tampoe in a 1993 research paper defined four stages in the career development of the knowledge worker as:

1. *Fulfilment* – a high sense of personal worth and job satisfaction derived from a balance of motivations (see diagram on the following page).
2. *Transitional* – arrived at a crossroads and is seeking to reposition: could happen at any time but more likely in late thirties or mid forties.

3. *Developmental* – a period of seeking equilibrium or balance of motivations: apart from the initial development stage and second stage, can occur in the late twenties or early thirties.
4. *Plateaued* – their career now meets their needs and they are unlikely to be seeking new challenges: they may actually fear change.

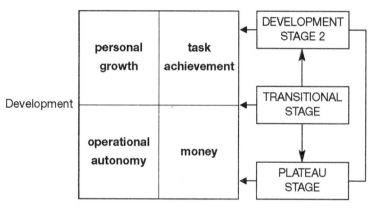

Fulfilment stage

Career path development stages

The four key motivations for the fulfilment stage above are:

1. *Personal growth* – individuals realise their potential in intellectual performance, personal relationships, career.
2. *Operational autonomy* – a work environment in which knowledge workers can achieve tasks without stress or hassle but within the organisational constraints.
3. *Task achievement* – the individual takes *pride* in work produced which is relevant to the organisation.
4. *Money* – amount earned is considered a just award for contribution and share in the wealth created.

In the diagram below we can see that the interplay of these stages and levels brings about different behaviour patterns. In the example we assume that the money level has reached the industry norm but the other motivations produce four distinct behaviours **A-D**:

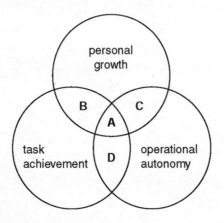

The four behaviour segments are:

A – *Fully motivated* behaviour

B – *Supervised* behaviour – which is acceptable to staff who see themselves in the development stage

C – *Employee centred* behaviour – the employee enjoys work but feels that they are not doing work that is really needed by the organisation; this behaviour fits the transitional stage

D – *Organisational centred* behaviour – excludes personal growth but meets the needs of the plateaued employee: a trade-off of personal growth for job security, often seen in older employees.

Building an effective environment

Mahan Tampoe's research included employee perceived management styles and practices which predominate in the current work environment and then identified eight requirements for building an effective knowledge management environment.

1 *Commercial relevance* – the assigned task is important to the business
2 *Task competence* – trained ability to carry out the task
3 *Task consistency* – stability in work so that energy is not constantly diverted to meet crisis or new initiatives
4 *Directed skills* – there is role clarity matched to skills and an opportunity to build new competencies
5 *Creative autonomy* – freedom to carry out the job without detailed supervision
6 *Resources* – sufficient tools available to do the job
7 *Commitment* – loyalty to the organisation rather than to specific colleagues or their profession
8 *Peer contacts* – access to relevant information and knowledge.

These can all be seen as instalments in enabling staff to perform well.

We can close Saturday with a summary of the five main requirements for achieving the best working environment for knowledge management and the learning organisation. They are:

- Motivated and committed workforce
- Individual competence

- Facilitative work environment
- Sense of purpose
- Genuine knowledge exchange

Conclusion

This week we have seen that introducing knowledge management requires a strong degree of commitment – from management and from all others involved. It takes time and resources. It needs a disciplined and systematic approach. It is enabled by information technology but it is a people rather than a technology dominated strategy.

In short, it is not easy and it is not for the faint-hearted. But then who has the right to believe that aiming and striving to be the best should ever be easy?

Further *Successful Business in a Week* **titles from Hodder & Stoughton and the Institute of Management all at £6.99**

0 340 71205 8	Appraisals in a Week	❏
0 340 70546 9	Assertiveness in a Week	❏
0 340 71197 3	Benchmarking in a Week	❏
0 340 57640 5	Budgeting in a Week	❏
0 340 74751 X	Bullying at Work in a Week	❏
0 340 72077 8	Business Growth in a Week	❏
0 340 70540 X	Business on the Internet in a Week	❏
0 340 71199 X	Business Plans in a Week	❏
0 340 62103 6	Business Process Re-engineering in a Week	❏
0 340 59813 1	Business Writing in a Week	❏
0 340 71200 7	Communication at Work in a Week	❏
0 340 62032 3	Computing for Business in a Week	❏
0 340 73781 6	Consultancy in a Week	❏
0 340 74752 8	Credit Control in a Week	❏
0 340 71196 5	Customer Care in a Week	❏
0 340 70543 4	CVs in a Week	❏
0 340 72076 X	Dealing with Difficult People in a Week	❏
0 340 63154 6	Decision Making in a Week	❏
0 340 73762 X	Delegation in a Week	❏
0 340 62741 7	Direct Mail in a Week	❏
0 340 73048 X	E-mail in a Week	❏
0 340 64330 7	Empowerment in a Week	❏
0 340 66374 X	Environmental Management in a Week	❏
0 340 71192 2	Finance for Non-Financial Managers in a Week	❏
0 340 71189 2	Flexible Working in a Week	❏
0 340 67925 5	Fundraising and Sponsorship in a Week	❏
0 340 71204 X	Going Freelance in a Week	❏
0 340 65487 2	Human Resource Management in a Week	❏
0 340 74287 9	Information Overload in a Week	❏
0 340 74756 0	Interviewing in a Week	❏
0 340 71179 5	Intranets in a Week	❏
0 340 63152 X	Introducing Management in a Week	❏
0 340 71203 i	Introduction to Bookkeeping and Accounting in a Week	❏
0 340 71202 3	Leadership in a Week	❏
0 340 71173 6	Management Gurus in a Week	❏
0 340 65503 8	Managing Change in a Week	❏

0 340 63153 8	Managing Information in a Week	❏
0 340 74757 9	Marketing in a Week	❏
0 340 47579 7	Marketing Plans in a Week	❏
0 340 57466 6	Market Research in a Week	❏
0 340 60894 3	Meetings in a Week	❏
0 340 74241 0	Memory Techniques in a Week	❏
0 340 61137 5	Mentoring in a Week	❏
0 340 71174 4	Mind Maps® in a Week	❏
0 340 73761 1	Motivation in a Week	❏
0 340 70545 0	Negotiating in a Week	❏
0 340 71123 X	Neuro-Linguistic Programming in a Week	❏
0 340 73812 X	Office Feng Shui in a Week	❏
0 340 72073 5	Personal Investment in a Week	❏
0 340 70541 8	Planning Your Own Career in a Week	❏
0 340 70544 2	Presentation in a Week	❏
0 340 71208 2	Process Management in a Week	❏
0 340 70539 6	Project Management in a Week	❏
0 340 64761 2	Problem Solving in a Week	❏
0 340 73780 8	Psychometric Testing in a Week	❏
0 340 56479 2	Public Relations in a Week	❏
0 340 71206 6	Purchasing in a Week	❏
0 340 61888 4	Quality Management Standards in a Week	❏
0 340 73816 2	Recruitment in a Week	❏
0 340 71198 1	Report Writing in a Week	❏
0 340 70538 8	Selling in a Week	❏
0 340 67397 4	Selling on the Internet in a Week	❏
0 340 65504 6	Statistics in a Week	❏
0 340 72494 3	Strategy in a Week	❏
0 340 71201 5	Stress Management in a Week	❏
0 340 70542 6	Succeeding at Interviews in a Week	❏
0 340 71207 4	Teambuilding in a Week	❏
0 340 70547 7	Time Management in a Week	❏
0 340 71191 4	Total Quality Management in a Week	❏
0 340 71195 7	Training in a Week	❏
0 340 62102 8	VAT in a Week	❏
0 340 67905 0	Virtual Organisation in a Week	❏
0 340 70508 6	Web Sites in a Week	❏

All Hodder & Stoughton books are available from your local bookshop or can be ordered direct from the publisher. Just tick the titles you want and fill in the form below. Prices and availability subject to change without notice.

To: Hodder & Stoughton Ltd, Cash Sales Department, Bookpoint, 39 Milton Park, Abingdon, Oxon, OX14 4TD. If you have a credit card you may order by telephone – 01235 400414.

E-mail address: orders@bookpoint.co.uk

Please enclose a cheque or postal order made payable to Bookpoint Ltd to the value of the cover price and allow the following for postage and packaging:

UK & BFPO: £4.30 for one book; £6.30 for two books; £8.30 for three books.

OVERSEAS & EIRE: £4.80 for one book; £7.10 for 2 or 3 books (surface mail).

Name: ....

Address: ....

....

If you would prefer to pay by credit card, please complete:

Please debit my Visa/Mastercard/Diner's Card/American Express (delete as appropriate) card no:

❏ ❏ ❏ ❏ ❏ ❏ ❏ ❏ ❏ ❏ ❏ ❏ ❏ ❏ ❏ ❏

Signature .... Expiry Date ....